Down Freedom Road

by
Hazel Clayton Harrison

Down Freedom Road

Copyright © 2020 by Hazel Clayton Harrison

All rights reserved. No part of this book may be reproduced or transmitted in any form or by any means without written permission of the author.

C. Jerome Woods, Consulting Editor

Library of Congress Control Number: 2019949792

ISBN: 978-0-9600931-2-0

Published by Shabda Press
Pasadena, CA 91107
www.shabdapress.com

Acknowledgments

Thanks to God for giving me inspiration to write. My deepest gratitude to my family and friends for their support and encouragement along my journey. To the International Black Writers & Artists, Pasadena for critiquing my drafts; to C. Jerome Woods for editing a final draft of my manuscript, and to Teresa Mei Chuc and Shabda Press for publishing my work. Without their talents and gifts this book would not be possible.

For our ancestors who made a way for us to follow

Contents

Harriet Tubman 1
The Drinking Gourd. 2
Frederick Douglass 3
Table Mountain. 4
I Am Woman 5
Blues for Lady Day 7
Ode To My Hips. 9
The Women Who Raised Me Up 10
Poem for Mother Harrison 12
Three Sisters 13
Learning to Compete 14
Dear Mama. 16
Love Letter to Grandpa 17
Portrait of My Father 18
For Daddy's Kin 19
Dear Country 20
Unemployed 21
Portrait of An Indian Grandmother. 22
Disappointment. 23
Love Equation. 24
Death On Del Monte 25
Hunger Moon. 26
Red Moon. 27
A Poet Warrior 28
9/11 29
Hands Up Don't Shoot!. 30
Freedom Road. 31
Words and Deeds Do Matter 32
Haenyeo Women of the Sea 33
A Little Watering 35

Tundra Bloom 36
Mystery Lover 37
Happy Hour 38
With Open Hearts And Hands 39
Avec Les Bras Et Les Coeurs Ouverts 40
Lil Woo's Eulogy for His Mama 42
When Death Visits 43
Altar of Stones 44
Sand Drawing 45
Daylight Savings Time 46
Lessons From An Evergreen 47
Eye of the Beholder 48
The Only Way You Can Leave 49
Under an Awning of Jacarandas 50
Sonny 52
His Eye is on the Sparrow 54
Ginny's Going Home 55
Lost and Found 56
Meditation on a Super Moon 57
Winter Haiku 58
What Freedom Means to Me 59
Folklore and Memoir 61
Uncle Cal 63
Saturday Cartoon Matinee 70
Blood on the Commons, The Kent State Massacre 72
One Day at the Black and Latino Bookstore 76
Hwange Sunset 78

References 81

Oh, Lord, I want to be free; rainbow round my shoulder, wings on my feet.

- African American spiritual

Harriet Tubman

Big Dipper
North Star
slave song risin'
pitch-black night
she be comin'
comin' like a seed pushin' up
comin' like North wind blowin' South
shadow risin'
gun barrel 'tween the eyes
blade razor sharp
cut bleedin'
night train runnin'
Better get on board
Be free or die, she say
Be free or die.

The Drinking Gourd

All I know about the stars
I learned from Harriet
Fix yo' eyes on the Big Dipper, she say

Follow the handle of that ole' drinkin' gourd
'til you sees the North Star

Follow it 'cross the river
If you hear dogs barkin', keep goin'

If you see torches burnin', keep goin'
Don't stop 'til you reach freedom land.

Frederick Douglass

When the master caught his missus
teaching me to spell, he said

Teach a nigger to read
and there'll be no keeping him

So I tricked the little white boys
of Baltimore into teaching me

For a crust of bread they gave me
the bread of knowledge

It was a fair trade
Because once I learned to spell

F-R-E-E-D-O-M

it stayed on my mind.

Table Mountain

(for Nelson Mandela)

Table Mountain stretches across the Cape of Good Hope
17 ½ kilometers across from Robben Island

where imprisoned Xhosa kings and warriors
gazed from between iron bars at the sacred table
around which they once sat

Hearing African drums
remembering the blood soaked soil
they yearned for their lost kingdoms

but in their hearts they knew
someday the table would turn and they would tear
down the walls of apartheid

to take back their rightful seats
at the head of the table.

I Am Woman

I am woman proud, black, and free
I am woman, extraordinary

In spite of hands that have tried to hold me down
      I have risen to mountain peaks

When my children were enslaved
      I stole across the Mason-Dixon line and led
      hundreds of slaves to freedom

When men denied my womanhood
      I tore open my blouse and declared
      Ain't I a woman?

When my children groped in darkness
      I founded schools and colleges

When charred black bodies hung from poplars
      in Tennessee, I became a journalist
      and used my pen as a weapon

When aviation was in its infancy
      I became a pilot and flew high
      above the clouds

I sang spirituals at the Lincoln Memorial
      and was received by lords and ladies
      in London and Liverpool

I am Harriet Ross Tubman
Sojourner Truth
Mary McLeod Bethune
Ida B. Wells
Bessie Coleman
Marian Anderson

I am woman, proud, black, and free
I am woman, extraordinary.

Blues for Lady Day

The blues
The blues

in all shades and hues
rose from the bottom
of the Mississippi
on bridges, barges, bayous
and bales of cotton

The blues
Down home blues
Sugar cane alley blues
I ain't got no shoes blues
I just got laid off blues
My man done left me blues

The blues
swept north on a train
on the chords of Miles Davis
and John Coltrane

Blew into Chicago
New York, Detroit, L.A.

It was in all the news
and somewhere among the blues
Sam Cooke sang
A change is gonna come

While B.B. King played Lucille
Billie Holiday sang the blues
lived the blues, was the blues
and the day she died

a new born baby cried
the blues.

Ode To My Hips

These hips have swayed across dim lit rooms
danced beneath silver stars and scarlet moons

Fought wars from Angola to Mali
Conquered kingdoms, carried nations across the sea

These hips have hypnotized men on every continent
When Europeans laid eyes on them, they rushed home
to create bustles for their women

On royal thrones these hips have been seated
Pharoahs and kings have bowed at their feet
These hips have birthed babies of every color

of the rainbow and raised them to be strong
These hips have been immortalized in stories and song

Like mountains these hips have endured earthquakes and storms
Gaze on them and be transformed.

The Women Who Raised Me Up

They weren't helpless, timid, take-care-of-me kind of women
They were fierce, strong, keep-goin-on women

Women who worked from sun up to sun down
along side grown men

Women who married young and birthed babies, not in hospitals
but in cotton fields or cabins

Women who learned to read and write in one room school houses

Women who rose before dawn to pack lunches and fix breakfasts
before heading to work as cooks, nannies, maids, and seamstresses

Women who sent their children to school to get the knowledge they were denied
Women who never took a day off from work

Who cleaned their own houses on Saturdays, went to church on Sundays
and came home to cook Sunday dinners from scratch

Women who didn't let their men push them around

Women who never went to counseling, but sat around kitchen tables
with girlfriends telling their stories

Laughing, crying, singing, smoking, dancing
to the records of Sam Cooke and Bobby "Blue" Bland

Women who refused to be crushed by heels of oppression
But stood up in city halls and PTA meetings, and marched to polls

No, they weren't helpless, timid, take-care-of-me kind of women
They were fierce, strong, keep-goin-on women.

Poem for Mother Harrison

Tower of strength, lighthouse of hope
wellspring of love and inspiration
mother to all who landed on her doorstep

No matter who you were, pauper or prince
she'd welcome you into her home, her heart

Cooked sumptuous meals from scratch
salmon, fresh asparagus, dinner rolls
and served them on silver, crystal, and china

If you stayed the night, she'd tuck you in with quilts
made with her own two hands

Roses and gladiolas bloomed wherever she walked
A gardener, cook, traveler, teacher, wisewoman
breath, song, prayer

Like her quilts, hand stitched
God doesn't make them like her any more.

Three Sisters

Corn   beans   squash
three companion
crops growing together
in the yard

Me   big sister
a corn stalk
tall   spindly
steadily reaching for sky
a pole for beans to climb

Middle sister
a string bean
eager to climb giving her juices
to help us grow

Little sister
yellow crookneck squash
vines spreading low
protecting   preventing weeds
from choking us

Three sisters
growing together
in the yard.

Learning to Compete

While sitting on the back porch
I watched the boys play baseball
There was my older brother Will
and Reuben, Skipper, and Paul

How I wished I could be a boy
So I could join in their sport
but they refused to let me play
Said I should stay on the porch

But when Skipper hit the ball
It flew over a neighbor's fence
I saw my chance to prove I could
match their strength and confidence

The chain-link fence was eight feet tall
But I climbed it like a pro
And when the boys laughed and cheered
I thought I was their super hero

But as I began to climb down
my shoulder began to hurt
My foot missed a link and I fell
right down into the dust and dirt

When Mama heard me wailing
She came running and took me home
She checked my back and shoulder
To make sure I hadn't broke a bone

Then she wiped my tears and said
Girls can't beat boys in their games
by climbing fences or running bases
but by exercising their brains

After that in boys' little leagues
I no longer tried to succeed
Instead, I learned to read and write
And conquered them with ease.

Dear Mama

This morning a yellow flower blossomed
from the prickly pear on the back porch

Its petals unfolded so gracefully
from its bed of thorns. I couldn't help
but think of you.

Love Letter to Grandpa

In that old sepia photo, you look
so handsome dressed in your Sunday-go-to-meeting suit
Your face, solemn as a Baptist preacher
Handle bar moustache trimming your upper lip
Eyes looking forward as if they could see the storms ahead.

Now I know why Big Mama fell
in love with you. For her, your tough, tender hands
dug up barrels of Georgia clay, turned them
into bales of cotton, reached up
plucked stars from the sky, stroked the moon.

Mama said when you prayed, angels wept
and heavens parted. The year before my
seed sprouted from her garden your long legs
leaped over rainbows, crossed the River Jordan
and headed home to Calvary.

Now I grow in ground you plowed, weeded,
planted. I never sat on your lap, or
called you Grandpa but one day we'll meet and
walk hand-in-hand into the rising sun.

Portrait of My Father

Faded blue trousers
Suspenders

Tweed cap covering
a brown moon head
Whiskers

Smell of bourbon and cigarettes
hands carved from thirty years
in steel

He now enjoys fishing
hunting and playing
with his grandchildren.

For Daddy's Kin

For Daddy's kin I never knew
For Grandpa John & Grandma Iona
For my uncles John, Henry & Lil Boy
For my aunts Katie, Ella Mae, & Doll

For their chopping, hoeing, picking, digging,
plowing, sowing, planting, pruning, hunting,
fishing, butchering, washing, ironing, cooking,
sewing, teaching, preaching, praying & enduring

On their shoulders I stand!
On their wings I fly!

Dear Country

(for Ron Jackson)

Sunlight breaking through clouds of gray
couldn't have brought me more joy
than the smile on your face

when unexpectedly, you sailed
into my hospital room

How did you know I was drowning in a
sea of sorrow?

Your hand, a life preserver for me to hold.

Unemployed

Behind corporate walls where she
pounded keyboards, answered phones
organized offices with computer-like efficiency
they said her skin was too black

She never got rid of her Kansas City drawl
No matter how good she was
she didn't fit the corporate image

So after working ten years for the same company
she found herself unemployed and facing the reality
that no one would hire an aging black queen
with no college degree

Too young for social security
too proud for welfare
she moved back to Kansas

Last I heard she was doing hair
and her blood pressure ain't as high
as it used to be.

Portrait of An Indian Grandmother

Her face is round
tanned as a leather pouch
Skin is parched
cracked like the Mojave
Eyes shine like stars
full of love, wisdom, truth
Hair soft as corn silk
Like the earth
she is beautiful.

Disappointment

      i don't know
which way

      the wind blows
anymore

      dead leaves rustle
broken promises

      under my feet.

Love Equation

Math was simple then. You
plus me equaled one. With
you I became whole.

I understood the meaning
of yin and yang, cause and
effect, earth, and sky

Don't good things come in pairs?
Then you left just when I
thought I had it all figured out

Now two minus one
equals nothing no matter
how I subtract.

Death On Del Monte

(in memory of Michael James Bryant)

Jacaranda petals purple sidewalks
Evening falls, a cloak

In front of the barber shop his friends and
family gather

To them he was a father, a son, a barber
who gave free haircuts to poor school boys

To the police who tased and hog-tied him
he was just another nigger

On Del Monte Street candles flicker
Shadows fall like footsteps leaving

The moon sheds…silver tears.

Hunger Moon

In February
hunger moon rises
on her haunches
rib cage lean
eyes yellow   bright
she creeps down
the mountain side
silent   haunting
the alleys
of night.

Red Moon

(for Rodney King)

Red moon hangin' in a dark sky
Red moon can you tell me why?
Red moon why you look so sad?
Red moon why am I treated so bad?

I was drivin' down the street
takin' my lady out to eat
when I heard the sirens wail
Next thing I knew I was whipped
and thrown in jail.

Red moon hangin' in a dark sky
Red moon can you tell me why?
Red moon why you look so sad?
Red moon why am I treated so bad?

A Poet Warrior

(for Ken Wibecan)

High yellow on the outside
black on the inside
working at newsroom desks all week
he hid his face behind Clark Kent glasses
writing stories about crack houses

gang violence and police brutality
But on weekends, he'd take
off his designer suit
don a dashiki, kufi, and
a necklace of cowrie shells

A poet warrior
he swept into our midst
spinning poems
awakening our
minds from illusions

of candy-cane-cadillac
white-picket-fence dreams
the plastic-polyester
Hollywood lies we'd been
spoon fed

Challenging us to look deeper within
and learn to love what's inside our own
black and beautiful skin.

9/11

Early morning wake up call
I turn on the TV
The sky is falling

watch the Twin Towers crumble
into pillars of smoke and dust

I was and I wasn't there
It was an out of body experience

I watched events unfold
from outer space

Went to work
I'm sure I spoke

I don't remember to whom
or what was said

But I recall tears falling
down my face

In a corner church
I held hands with strangers
and prayed.

Hands Up Don't Shoot!

We raise our hands
but it don't matter

POW! POW! POW!
Bullets fly

We run
Trey fall down
I hear his mama cry

Hands up don't shoot!

In movies hands up
means surrender

Cops handcuff rebels
take them to jail

But for us the same rules
don't apply

Whether our hands
are up or down
we die.

Freedom Road

Jim Crow laws . . . Charred black bodies . . . Strange fruit
Hung from southern trees

American flag . . . Drenched in blood . . . Sick and tired
Black Migration . . . Escape from terror

Harlem Nights . . . Weary blues . . . Lift every voice
March on Washington . . . Freedom fighters . . . Voter registration

Many rivers to cross . . . Hurricane Katrina . . . Black folks left to drown
Mother Emanuel . . . Blood on the cross

First Black president . . . Amazing Grace . . . Voices echo down halls
White backlash . . . Charlottesville, Virginia . . . Encroaching shadows

Tiki torches . . . Hate & terrorism . . . Dark brew of troubles
Homelessness . . . Wolves eat babies . . . Strange the stars

Press on children . . . Taste freedom . . . Hear the dawn birds sing.

Words and Deeds Do Matter

So unbecoming of a man your age
a man of great wealth, power, and fame
To strut out on the world stage
And preach hate like it's but a children's game

Like a rooster you puff your chest and crow
about the women you've sexually molested
Makes me wonder how much lower can you go
For your crimes a poor man would be arrested!

You say it's all just locker room talk
But decent honest men don't boast that way
Your foul mouth has made you a laughing stock
Your voice sounds like an asses' bray

No one wants to listen to a president so bitter
he tweets all his fears and woes on Twitter.

Haenyeo Women of the Sea

(for mothers who make great sacrifices to educate their daughters)

For generations they were the bread winners of
    Jeju Island

Without breathing gear, they dove into the Korea
    Strait holding their breaths, harvesting seafood

Poor and illiterate, they swam like fish in schools
    carrying their coffins on their backs*

Under her blue-green waves, Mother Sea nourished them
    with her abalone and algae

When pregnant, the sea women dreamed of delivering
    their babies in Mother Sea's arms

In times of sorrow, salt from their tears mingled with hers
    When Seoulmundae** heard them weeping

she spilled lava over the island until school officials
    opened their doors for her daughters

The sea women had to dive deeper to pay school fees
    but now their daughters are educated

And they do not have to dive carrying coffins
    on their backs

The sea women are now grandmothers. Soon they will
    disappear, but today they still plunge into the sea

holding their breaths, harvesting seafood, happy to
    sink into Mother Sea's embrace.

*Phrase the Haenyeo use to describe net sacks they carry on their backs when diving
**Mother Creator, the Haenyeo's name for Mount Halla

A Little Watering

Sometimes all we need is
a little watering
just a little watering

An old cactus dying in the yard
Watered it one day
and you should've seen how it bloomed
You should've seen how it bloomed!

Went to visit my brother after many years
Deep talk and laughter healed our wounds
and dried our tears

The sun is shining bright today
Yesterday it rained
Flowers are blooming everywhere
Everywhere!

All they needed was a little watering
just a little watering.

Tundra Bloom

From coast to coast I've seen
the world's finest heirlooms
but never have I seen one
more lovely than a tundra bloom

Planted in soil, rich and fertile
tended by a gardener's hand
the heirloom blossom's beauty
is sung throughout the land

But pushing up from mountain
sides the tundra bloom rises
with velvet petals so vibrant
the eye it hypnotizes

From coast to coast I've seen
the world's finest heirlooms
but never have I seen one
more lovely than a tundra bloom.

Mystery Lover

After a long day at work
I climb in my car and drive fifty miles
in rush hour traffic

As I reach my exit
my heartbeat quickens

I am getting closer to the moment
I've been waiting for all day

I park my car, open the door and
rush into the bedroom
to find you still lying on the bed

Quickly, I pull off my clothes
climb under the covers
crawl next to you
caress your spine

Licking my lips
I open you
and devour every word.

Happy Hour

With twenty-four hours in a
day why is only one reserved
for happiness?

Five o'clock! A bell rings. Ding!
Like birds we flock to a watering

hole to guzzle half-priced drinks,
laugh, and sing until an alarm
sounds. Ding! Time to go home and
be unhappy.

Why can't happiness last all day
or at least for more than just
one hour?

With Open Hearts And Hands

Welcome! Welcome!
Brothers and Sisters of Dakar-Plateau, Senegal
Welcome to Pasadena, Crown of the Valley

We welcome you with baskets of flowers
lilies, lilacs, poppies, and roses
We welcome you with baskets of fruit
strawberries, grapes, peaches, and plums

We welcome you with art, song, and dance
We welcome you with business, science, technology
We welcome you with open hearts and hands

We are proud of our cultural diversity
Some of us are descendants of Native Californians
Most of us are descendants of people from distant lands
But we are all Americans rooted in America's shores and sands

We are entrepreneurs, engineers, educators
doctors, lawyers, artists, and administrators
Today, we welcome you, our newest sister city
In every language sister has the same meaning

It means sharing natural and cultural resources
It means honoring and respecting one another
It means lending a helping hand
It means growing in peace, love, and understanding

With open arms, we welcome you to our city
We welcome you into our hearts, our homes
May our sisterhood flower and be fruitful.

Avec Les Bras Et Les Coeurs Ouverts

(French Translation of *With Open Hearts and Hands*)

Bienvenue! Bienvenue!
Frères et Soeurs de Dakar-Plateau, du Senegal
Bienvenue à Pasadena, Couronne de la Vallée de Saint Gabriel

Nous vous accueillons avec des gerbes de fleurs
Avec des lys, des lilacs, des coquelicots et des roses
Nous vous accueillons avec des paniers pleins de fruits
Pleins de fraises, de raisins verts, de pèches, de prunes

Nous vous accueillons avec notre Art, nos chansons, et nos danses
Nous vous accueillons avec nos industries, nos avancées économiques
Nos découvertes scientifiques, nos progrès techniques, notre système Educatif
Nous vous accueillons avec le cœur et les bras ouverts

Nous sommes fiers de la diversité culturelle de notre ville
Nous sommes d'un peu partout, des Natifs de la Californie même,
Descendants de peuples nombreux venant de pays lointains,
pourtant tous Américains
Notre histoire et nos destinées ancrées dans le sable de cette Amérique

Nous sommes des Entrepreneurs, des Ingénieurs, des Professeurs
Nous sommes Médecins, Avocats, Artistes, Politiciens
Nous sommes Hommes et Femmes d'Affaire, Ecrivains, Poètes et Peintres
Aujourd'hui, nous vous disons Bienvenue, vous, notre nouvelle ville-Sœur

Sœurs, ayant à partager nos ressources tant naturelles que culturelles
Appelées à nous respecter l'une l'autre, à nous tendre la main, à nous entre aider
Sœurs, appelées à grandir en paix, en compréhension et en amour

Avec les bras ouverts, nous vous accueillons dans notre ville
Nous vous faisons place dans nos cœurs, nous vous ouvrons les portes de nos maisons
Que notre collaboration fleurisse et sois toujours fructueuse

Lil Woo's Eulogy for His Mama

(inspired by Dawud Abdullah)

da angel of death
called mama home last week

but I'm at peace wid dat
she got ninety-five good years n

did her own thang
had her own place

grew her own greens
bought her own pearls

drove her own caddie
on da highway
at 55 miles an hour

raised all five of us
me bein' da baby
and da baddest

she tore my butt up
taught me to drive
on da hardest roads.

When Death Visits

He will not leave, even after the funeral
Dressed in a cloak of sorrow
he will linger in your rooms

listening to your weeping and wailing
watching you roam the halls in slippers and robe

If you sit beside him he will tell you
of all the good things he brings
peace and release from pain and suffering

Like a teacher he will review your report card
telling you whether you are passing or failing
subjects in the Book of Life

But he will not leave until your tears stop overflowing
and your heart fills with knowing that love never dies.

Altar of Stones

At the library
behind a brick wall
beneath shadows of evergreens

a conservation garden
       slopes down
              a winding trail

Pine cones nestle in its nooks
Butterflies dance on its sweet breath
Baby blue eyes open under its shade

Like a bird song the garden beckons weary travelers
Come sit by my side

Lay your books on my bed of pine needles
Listen to wind play my chimes

Rest your eyes on cloves of purple and gold
Heal your broken hearts with my fragrance
of sage and mimulus

Leave your worries on my altar of stones.

Sand Drawing

One day I watched a sect of Buddhist monks
draw a mandala made of colored sands

With skillful hands, they drew gardens, temples
designs so divine, like stars in the heavens
they shined

When the monks were done, to my dismay
one took a brush and swept it all away

When I asked him what that meant
he smiled and said, *Existence is impermanent*

Now when I look at my house, my car
my reflection in a looking glass

I remember what that wise man said
Someday they will all pass.

Daylight Savings Time

Can we really save daylight?
Put it in a bag

One made of lead, not plastic
so it won't leak out

And what to do with
that extra hour in spring?

Save it for a rainy day
when clouds are gray

Or put it in a vault at the bank
When time falls back, exchange it
like currency

I wish I could preserve mine in a honey jar
and sip it with chamomile tea.

Lessons From An Evergreen

Along
the road
I met an old evergreen
Her crown brushed the sky
her trunk forked into three
her roots coiled deep into the soil
Chile, where you goin in such a hurry
Why don't you stop and rest a spell?
"Sorry, I ain't got time," I said pausing to admire her odd shape
A blue jay landed on one of her limbs
She listened to its chatter then focused her eyes on me
Sometimes you get more done bein' still than you do runnin' 'round
I been standin' in this same spot for over a hundred years and I bet
I get mo' done in one hour than you do in a whole life time
Her trunk invited me to sit and her pine scent cleared my head
Just 'cause y'all don't hear trees talk don't mean we can't
We got all kinds of phone lines underground
Know how I make it through a storm?
I let go of dead branches so I can bend in the wind
Sometimes you gotta let thangs go
I sat for a while listening
to the woosh of wind
whispering
in her leaves
Heading home
I realized
I learned more
from her
in one hour
than I learned from
all my years in school.

Eye of the Beholder

Why should I long for the beauty
of my younger self?

for the fairness of her complexion
the firmness of her thigh?

Does the ripened apple long
for the blossom from which it sprang?

Does the oak long for the acorn
from which it was born?

Does the full moon lament
the waxing of her crescent?

Life is all metamorphosis
Transformation from chrysalis
to butterfly

For the beauty of my younger self
why should I weep?

Why should I cry?

The Only Way You Can Leave

It is easier for a camel to go through the eye of a needle than for a rich man to enter into the kingdom of God (Matthew 19:24, King James Bible)

Don't envy the rich!

The rich man has many mansions with empty rooms
but refuses to house the poor.

The homeless woman shares her crust of bread
with strangers.

With whom would you want to go to bow before the Lord?
Don't envy the rich!

The only way you can leave this house
is empty handed.

Under an Awning of Jacarandas

Under an awning of jacarandas
we danced, dreamed, laughed, and played

Under an awning of jacarandas
our first child was born

We cradled him in our arms
strolled him down purple lanes

Under an awning of jacarandas
we celebrated birthdays, holidays

On the 4th of July we watched fireworks
explode in a violet sky

Under an awning of jacarandas
seasons changed

leaves withered and died
dreams fell, a purple rain

Under an awning of jacarandas
We broke each others' hearts

Our marriage fell apart
We went separate ways

Now in spring when
jacaranda petals fall

I think of you and all
the memories recalled.

Sonny

Sonny was old school, the type of man
who didn't stand out in a crowd but you
knew he was there

A man who liked to work with his hands
He fixed his own cars
grew his own vegetables

He even made his own wine
We called it Sonniac

Every now and then he'd show up at
my back door with a bag of collard greens
and a bottle of Sonniac

In the kitchen we'd sip his wine and talk
about old times

When he left, I'd cook the greens
laughing about some story he'd told

The last time he came by he brought sad news
I got lung cancer. Doctor says I got 3 months left
We sat quiet for a long time that day

The next week I went by his house
He stopped working in his yard long
enough to pour me a glass of Sonniac

I sipped it slowly
The taste still lingers sweet
on my tongue.

His Eye is on the Sparrow

(for my brother, Willie)

After hymns were sung, prayers were said
testimonies were spoken, and scriptures read

Feet marching in time with the seasons
the sisters three most solemnly
made a procession through the cemetery

Carrying their brother's ashes in a box
and purple violets in plastic pots
they passed manicured lawns and monuments of stone

until they reached the colored section
where their parents had been laid to rest

Kneeling beside an empty patch, they dug a hole
spread his ashes, and planted violets on top

Then an incredible sight caught the older sister's eye
On a grassy knoll, a red tail hawk lifted its wings
and took to the sky.

Ginny's Going Home

Ginny's skin, translucent, pale as a new moon
She could have passed for white, but always claimed
her Indian blood

When she died her husband, Leon, planted a tree
in her honor. At the memorial Bobby Bluejacket burned
white sage and waved eagle feathers

While Leon spread her ashes around the sapling elm
wind whispered *Ginny, Ginny, Ginny* through eucalyptus leaves

As we read poetry in a garden of lilies, lilacs, and roses
a good omen, an eagle appeared and circled the sky

In jubilation, we waved and shouted
Good-bye, Ginny, Good-bye!

Lost and Found

Far and wide, I've traveled this foreign land
Seeking a place to lay my weary breast
Passing valleys where my kind have been banned
Hoping to find a grove where I can rest.

At times I wonder if my life's been cursed
To ease the fears and troubles in my mind
I've read the Bible chapter, line, and verse
Nowhere does it say God is colorblind.

So low I've fallen my head bows in shame
I want to jump in a river and drown
But then I hear the Lord calling my name
Telling me I've been lost and now I'm found.

Now I know my home is where'er I am
He is my shepherd and I am His lamb.

Meditation on a Super Moon

Oh, supermoon hanging so large
and luminous in the sky I gaze at you
and wonder.

Are you a lantern made to light the way
for ships lost at sea?

Or, the lens of a great telescope from
a distant galaxy?

Or, are you Earth's faithful lover
come to bathe her tonight
in your ineffable light?

Winter Haiku

Coltrane's Love Supreme
drifting over street lamps
      Memories of home.

November sunrise
Crowning Mount Baldy's peak
      a misty halo.

A foggy morning
Old opossum peers through cage bars
      What did he do wrong?

Indigo sky
Venus shines like diamonds
      on the moon's finger.

Super blood wolf moon
What omens do you foretell?
      Those whispering pines.

What Freedom Means to Me

F is for flight. To spread my wings and let go of all the limitations society places on me.

R is for responsibility. To take responsibility for my words, thoughts, and deeds. To have respect for all life and obey Nature's laws of giving and receiving.

E is for evolve. To evolve into my higher self and become the person I was meant to be. To find my purpose and use it to help make the world a better place.

E is for eternal. To be guided by the eternal force that keeps celestial bodies in motion, and activates every atom in my body.

D is for divine. To connect my divinity to the Divine Spirit that lights the heavens.

O is for openness. To open my heart to the power of Love, and my mind to the unlimited possibilities that exist for the future.

M is for mystery. To ponder the mysteries of the universe with the understanding that I will never have all the answers.

Folklore and Memoir

Uncle Cal

Uncle Cal lived ten miles down the road from Hattie Mae. She had never been to his house, but had seen him many times heading down the road toward town; his figure, tall, dark, and bent like an old fig tree. Whenever she saw him, she hid behind the barn and watched him go by. She could never figure out what it was about him that frightened her. Perhaps it was the way his head bent forward, bobbing up and down in time with the horses. Or the way his coattail flapped like the wings of a giant bird. Or maybe, it was the stories she'd heard about him.

Stories about Uncle Cal spread through Hopeful, Georgia like love bugs in spring. Some said he had magical powers and could cure diseases with roots and herbs. Some said he had once raised a man from the dead. Supposedly, old Sam had been shot by the sheriff for stealing watermelons from Mr. Carter's plantation. The sheriff had called his wife to come and get his body. In desperation, she had taken the body to Uncle Cal's. Lo and behold, Sam was seen riding beside his wife in their wagon the next day.

Hattie Mae wasn't sure she believed any of the stories about Uncle Cal, but she knew there was something strange about him. She was determined to keep her distance until she met Jake Wesley that is.

She had never known a man like Jake. He had lived up North in New York for the last eight years and had come home to stay with his Aunt Jessie. Some said he was hiding from the law, but Hattie Mae ignored the gossip.

She met him on one of her trips to town to buy supplies. "Oou, wee!" he said, stepping out of the General Store. "If you ain't the prettiest thang south of the Mason-Dixon line, I'll be a coon's ass."

His sudden outburst had caused a blush to creep up the sides of her face. She dropped her head in embarrassment, and almost tripped down the steps as she headed toward her wagon. She tried to ignore him, but he fell into step behind her.

"Say, Miss, whas yo' name? Can I have the pleasure of buyin' you a soda?"

She blushed again and began loading her goods into the wagon.

"Here lemme help you," he said, stepping forward and taking a twenty pound sack of flour from her arms. Just then Big John, Hattie Mae's grandfather, showed up. He shot Jake a mean look and ordered Hattie Mae into the wagon. Then he loaded the rest of the goods and took off without saying a word.

All over town Big John was known as a quiet man with a temper bad as a tornado. Even the sheriff cut a wide path around him.

All the way home Hattie Mae could not get Jake out of her mind. Perhaps it was the way he wore his hair slicked back with pomade. Or was it his smooth, honey brown skin? Or the even whiteness of his teeth? Whatever it was, it had taken hold of her like a honeysuckle wrapped around a tree and would not let her go.

The next week she jumped at the chance to go into town alone when her grandmother, Miss Pearl, asked her to buy some lye to make soap. This time she put on her best dress, the one covered with big yellow sunflowers. And she wore a wide-brimmed straw hat instead of the scarf she usually tied around her head.

"You git home fo' yo' grandpap gets back from the cane field," Miss Pearl said as Hattie Mae headed out the door. "You know how he frets over you."

When Hattie Mae got to town, Jake was leaning against a pole in front of the General Store.

"Good afternoon, Miss," he said as she walked by him, "I been comin' here every day since last week hopin' to run into you. I sure would likes to get to know you better. Would you mind if I come calling on you some evening?"

Hattie Mae's tongue twisted into a knot. So far the only boy who had ever come calling on her was Willie Boy, who was short and ugly with buck teeth. None of the girls at church liked him. Sometimes Hattie Mae would sit on the front porch with him, but she always kept her distance. Once he tried to kiss her when Big John wasn't looking. She had jumped up and run into the house, refusing to come out no matter how hard he begged.

But she had just turned fifteen and knew Big John would never approve of her seeing Jake. Ever since her mama ran off with a smooth city man right after she was born, Big John had distrusted all men. He refused to let any boy come near her, except Willie Boy. And the only reason he let Willie Boy come calling was because he knew she disliked him.

Hattie Mae explained to Jake that Big John would never consent to having him come calling on her, but she offered to meet him outside of town. Even she was surprised at her boldness, offering to meet a stranger on a lonesome road. After finishing her shopping, she jumped in the wagon. She had barely gone a mile when she spotted Jake sitting under an oak tree. She parked the wagon and he helped her climb down.

They walked down the hill a bit and talked. He told her that he moved to Hopeful to help his Aunt Jessie on the farm. Soon they were laughing and talking like old friends. Hattie Mae was fascinated by the stories he told about places in Harlem with fancy names like Lenox Avenue and Sugar Hill. He was the worldliest man she had ever known, not to mention the most handsome. That afternoon they spent a short time together, but agreed to meet again the next week. Soon they were meeting weekly.

One day he asked her to meet him late that evening near Coon's Creek. Hattie Mae agreed only after he promised her he would not keep her out long. He said he had something important to tell her.

That night while Miss Pearl and Big John snored loudly, Hattie Mae tiptoed out the house and ran down to the creek. Jake was waiting there for her. He looked even more handsome, his face aglow in the moonlight. "I want you to be my wife," he said, when they had settled on the ground under a sweet gum tree.

"But what about all those pretty ladies in Harlem?" Hattie Mae teased.

"What ladies?" The look on his face turned serious. His eyes caressed her face. He leaned forward and scooped her in his arms.

Swept away by the moonlight, the warmth of his arms encircling her, the scent of his body, she weakened. Before she knew it, she was lying on her back and he was on top of her. As they lay beneath the stars, a frog croaked. A dog howled. Crickets played a symphony. Wind tickled the leaves. Later Hattie Mae crept back into the house and crawled into bed. She was under his spell now more than ever.

After that night there were many clandestine trips to Coon's Creek. One morning when Miss Pearl was fixing grits, eggs, and fatback, Hattie Mae bolted from the table and ran outside. She could not stand the smell of fatback frying in the pan. She barely made it outside before she threw up. She was leaning over the side of the rail when Miss Pearl came outside.

"Whas wrong with you, gal?" Miss Pearl demanded.

"I don't know Mother Pearl. I just felt poorly all of a sudden. I must have a touch of the flu."

Miss Pearl's eyes bore a hole in Hattie Mae's. "You ain't been messin' with that new fella I heared about?"

"Naw Mother Pearl, what make you think somethin' like that?" Hattie Mae's eyes grew big and round as a robin's eggs.

"Don't lie to me, gal!" Miss Pearl's hand shot out and slapped Hattie Mae across the face. "I knows when a gal's in a family way. I just hope and pray Big John don't find out."

The words had barely come out of Miss Pearl's mouth when Big John appeared in the doorway.

"Hope I don't find out what?" he demanded. Big John's eyes traveled from Miss Pearl's face to Hattie Mae's swollen jaw. Then a storm brewed in them.

"That no good dog," he growled, "I'll kill him." Without uttering another word, he turned and strode into the back room. When he returned, he was carrying his double-barreled shotgun

Everyone knew Big John was a man of few words and quick action. So, Hattie Mae and Miss Pearl knew he meant business.

"Now Big John, put that gun down fo' you do something foolish." Miss Pearl stood in his way.

With one arm, he brushed her aside and strode toward the barn. Hattie Mae ran after him pleading and crying. But he ignored her and kept on walking. He hitched his wagon to a horse and took off down the road like he was chasing the devil himself.

Hattie Mae stood in the middle of the road stricken with hurt and grief. Suddenly, she knew she had to warn Jake. The wagon Big John used to take Hattie Mae and Miss Pearl to church was sitting on the side of the barn. In no time, Hattie Mae had it hitched to Fanny, the old mare they used to plow the fields, and took off after Big John.

She knew just where to find Jake. He usually spent his afternoons sitting in front of Pete's Corner Store chewing the fat with the Jackson boys. She got there just after Big John rounded the corner. When the Jackson boys saw Big John heading toward them with his shotgun raised, they scattered like crows being chased from a corn field. But Jake, who had been sitting on a stool near the door, did not move fast enough. The last thing he heard was an explosion from Big John's shotgun.

The next thing anybody knew, Jake was lying in the middle of the road, a hole big as a fifty cent piece in his chest. Hattie Mae screamed and ran to him. Big John tried to stop her, but she tore loose from him and knelt beside Jake. No one doubted he was dead. His eyes had rolled to the back of his head, and blood poured from a gaping hole in his chest. There was nothing left to do but take him to old man Davis' funeral parlor.

When Big John left, the boys lifted Jake's body. Before they could place it on their wagon, Hattie Mae screamed, "No, put him in my wagon. I'll take him."

The men looked sheepishly at each other. No one said a word. They placed his body in Hattie Mae's wagon and watched as she headed toward the funeral parlor.

Hattie Mae was half way down the road when she struck upon an idea. She remembered the stories about Uncle Cal. What if he could help Jake? The idea terrified and compelled her at the same time. When she came to the fork in the road, she took the road that led to Uncle Cal's place.

Uncle Cal's shack stood in the middle of a thick underbrush a few miles outside of town. The sun had begun to set when Hattie Mae pulled her wagon up to his gate and stepped down. The shack looked as old as the hills with rotting wood siding, a rusted tin roof, and a front porch with steps that sagged from burdens that country folks brought to his doorstep.

At first she thought he wasn't home, but when she knocked on the door she heard footsteps.

"Who is it?" a voice asked from inside.

"It's Hattie Mae, Miss Pearl's granddaughter," she said.

The door opened and Uncle Cal stood in the doorway. He was just a little over five feet tall, smaller than Hattie Mae imagined with skin that looked like the bark of an old birch and patches of cotton growing from the sides of his head.

He peered at her suspiciously. "What you doin' out here this time a night? I 'spect this ain't no social visit," he muttered.

"No, Suh," Hattie Mae tried to hold back her tears, "I heard you could heal folks. I thought maybe you could help Jake. He been shot." She pointed toward the wagon.

Uncle Cal's cat eyes followed her finger. He stepped outside, went to the wagon, and stood there looking at Jake's body. His crooked middle fingers felt Jake's neck. Slowly, he climbed the porch stairs.

"That man's dead as a log," he said, shaking his head. "T'ain't nothin' I kin do for him."

"But I heard you had special powers. I thought you could save him."

Uncle Cal's eyes narrowed. "Chile, can't nobody raise the dead but Jesus. And Jesus, I ain't. Now if you'll 'scuse me, I was 'bout to fix muh supper."

He headed inside the house, but Hattie Mae grabbed his arm. "Uncle Cal, please!" she begged, "I'm expectin' his baby. If you don't save him, my baby won't have no daddy."

Uncle Cal stopped, turned, and scratched his head. He considered what she said for a moment.

"I ain't promisin' no miracles," he finally said, "but I'll see what I kin do."

Together they lifted Jake's body off the wagon and carried him into the house. They laid him on a cot in the back room. Uncle Cal told Hattie

Mae to wait in the front room, which was only big enough to hold a small table and a couple of straight back chairs. A worn croker sack curtain hung over the kitchen doorway.

Hattie Mae watched through the veil as Uncle Cal performed his magic. He moved in and out of candle light from the kitchen to the back room. In the kitchen, he boiled a pot of water. To the water, he added herbs from jars he kept in the cupboard. He then took the pot in the back room.

As Hattie Mae sat wringing her hands, she could hear him singing in a strange tongue. Hours later, he emerged through the curtain.

"You kin go in and see him now," he said, "But remember, he still weak from losin' blood."

Hattie Mae rushed through the curtain and found Jake lying on the cot, his chest covered with a thick bandage.

"Jake," she whispered, "Can you hear me?"

She sucked in her breath when his hand reached out and touched hers.

"Is that you, Baby?" he asked, opening his eyes. Hattie Mae could not believe it. Jake was alive!

She offered to come to work for Uncle Cal to pay him for bringing Jake back to life, but he refused, saying she should just bring the baby around to see him when he was born. Under a full blood moon, Hattie Mae and Uncle Cal lifted Jake into the wagon. As Fanny stomped her hoofs, Hattie Mae waved good-bye to Uncle Cal.

The next day one of the Jackson boys swore he saw Jake riding next to Hattie Mae in a buggy big as day. But they disappeared and were never seen or heard from again. Still, some say from time to time when the moon is full, they see them lying by the creek. Others say, they see Uncle Cal heading down a dirt road late at night with a small child riding by his side.

Saturday Cartoon Matinee

Summer of 1956. I am eight years old and excited to be sitting next to my brother Will in the back seat of our father's leaf green 1947 Dodge Fluid Drive. We're on our way to Georgia to visit my grandma. Behind the wheel Daddy looks like a pilot flying a plane and riding in the passenger's seat Mama is his co-pilot. It's a long drive from Ohio to Georgia. So Mama packed sodas, chips, and a brown paper bag full of her delicious fried chicken for us to eat along the way. As we ride down the highway there's a whole new world to see, mountains, lakes, rivers, streams, cows, horses, and valleys of green.

When we finally reach Big Mama's, I'm happy to see her but tired from riding in the car for so long. She lives out in the country on a farm. Her house is painted bright yellow and is surrounded by sunflowers and tall pines. But I sense there's something evil that lurks beneath the surface of the South. Maybe it's the water snakes that slither in ponds and lakes. Maybe it's the weather, the sun that bakes us like bread, or the way overripe watermelons lie in the field with pulp spilling out like guts from the dead. Maybe it's the God awful smell of the outhouse that leans in the back. Maybe it's the way Big Mama wrings a chicken's neck. The way the bird runs around the yard flapping its wings with its head dangling like a broken doll's.

I can't put my finger on what the thing is until Saturday when Mama gets tired of us being underfoot, and sends Will and me into town to a cartoon matinee. Will is ten, two years older than me. Usually we don't get along, but today I'm glad we're together because Mama told him he'd better take good care me. It's only a half mile into town, but the sun burns my skin like a hot iron.

The little theater slumps on Main Street next to a drug store. It is smaller and shabbier than the ones back home in Ohio, but to Will and me it is an oasis in the desert. At the box office, Will drops fifty cents for two tickets into the slot. Inside the lobby the air feels cold as an icebox. The popcorn smells delicious but we don't have a nickel to buy a bag. So we head past the concession stand toward the auditorium. As we near the door, an usher steps in front of us. He's an old bald headed guy with a puffy red face and gray eyes that match the color of his vest. He glares at us and says with a heavy Southern drawl, "The colored section's upstairs."

Gazing into his eyes, I wonder what a colored section is. Is it a special room for kids painted in bright colors? As we step behind the drapes at the top of the stairs, my palms start to sweat. The seats are all empty. The air smells musty as an old damp blanket. Holding on to an iron rail, I follow Will down the stairs and sit beside him in the front row. While waiting for the show to start, I look over the rail. As I stare into a sea of kids their heads bobbing like rubber ducks, it hits me. They're all white! Then I know what a colored section is. Closing my eyes, I sink into my seat. As I sit there trembling, I feel the little balloon tucked between my legs begin to swell. I don't want to tell Will I have to pee. But afraid I'm going to wet my pants, I whisper the bad news into his ear.

"Shit," Will curses, pushes himself up out of his seat, and orders me to follow him up the stairs. In the lobby the usher guards the door like an old pit bull. I hang back as Will approaches him. "Where's the girl's bathroom," he asks. I want to sink into the ground and disappear when the usher curls his lip and sneers, "Y'all must not be from here. There ain't no restrooms for coloreds in this town." My body goes numb. I choke back tears. In silence, we head down Main Street. When we reach the dirt road leading to Big Mama's, Will turns his back while I go behind a bush to pee. At Big Mama's house, we tell her and Mama what happened. They shake their heads and say they're sorry, but that's the way things are down South.

Blood on the Commons, The Kent State Massacre

A cold chill ran up my spine when I read headlines in the Thursday, April 30, 1970 edition of the Kent newspaper and saw that American troops were going to invade Cambodia. I knew the news would ripple across campus, creating a maelstrom.

Heading across campus at noon on Friday, I stopped to watch a crowd of several hundred students surrounding the Victory Bell. Donated to the university by the Erie Railroad in 1950, it was placed in a brick wall by Taylor Hall. Traditionally, the heavy iron toll was rung to celebrate homecoming game victories. Now it was used to signal the start of anti-war rallies.

Standing on a hill overlooking the bell, I watched a skinny red-haired student hold up a copy of the U.S. Constitution.

"Today we are burying the Constitution because Nixon murdered it when he sent troops into Cambodia without a congressional declaration," he shouted over a bullhorn.

The crowd cheered as he placed the foundation of American liberties into a hole and another student shoveled dirt over it. Fundamentally, I was against the war and hated Nixon. But it felt strange to watch the Constitution being buried. I wondered if the rights it was supposed to protect had also been murdered. As I turned to walk away, a pretty sandy haired girl handed me a flyer which announced that a rally would be held in front of the ROTC building on Saturday. I accepted the flyer but when the girl walked away, I wadded it up and tossed it in a trash barrel.

I had given birth to my daughter, Angela, the previous summer and couldn't afford to get caught up in student demonstrations. I had to graduate and get a job, so I could take care of my child.

On Friday afternoon I went home to spend the weekend helping Mama take care of Angela. At eight months, she was starting to walk and get into things. Each time I went home, I was amazed at how fast she was growing. Her rapid development was a steady reminder that I had to stay focused and graduate within the next two years.

On Sunday, I went back to campus glad to escape my parental duties for a while. But when I arrived, I felt like I had landed on the front lines of Vietnam. Armored vehicles and hundreds of troops guarded buildings all over campus. Hurrying across the commons, I noticed an army tank blocking the main entrance to the ROTC building. It was as big as a small dwelling with a huge cannon protruding from a turret. About a dozen young national guardsmen guarded it with M-1 rifles slung over their shoulders. They were young soldiers who didn't look much older than the students they were sent to battle.

Behind the combat vehicle stood the charred remains of the ROTC building. The acrid odor of tear gas and cinders burned my nostrils. The whole scene was eerie and ominous.

Feeling suddenly sick to my stomach, I ran to my apartment building. Inside, I listened to my roommates talk about the chain of events that had occurred over the weekend.

"I was there when it all started," Casey, a petite, dark-complexioned girl from Philadelphia said. She was an English major who usually enunciated every syllable. Now the words tripped off her tongue. "On Friday night we were downtown on Water Street partyin' 'til some bikers got drunk and started throwin' beer bottles at cars. Somebody started a bonfire in the middle of the street. I left when the vandalizing started."

"Yeah, it was awful," Diane, my roommate from Cleveland, interrupted her. She was tall and light skinned with long reddish brown hair. "There musta been a thousand students at the rally in front of the ROTC building on Saturday. At first they just stood around. Then somebody set the building on fire. While it burned, everybody cheered. It was like something out of the Twilight Zone." Her perfectly arched eyebrows knitted into a frown. "I hear there's gonna be another demonstration tomorrow. I think I'll stay here. Those soldiers look like they mean business."

That night I lay awake listening to helicopter blades beating the sky, trying to decide whether to stay home or go to class the next day. Part of me wanted to skip class and hide out in my apartment. On the other hand, it was the week of mid-terms. I needed to keep my grades up. My mother's words rang in my ears, *After you graduate, this baby will be all yours.* In the end, I decided to go to class.

Monday, May 4th dawned one of those beautiful, crisp, clear, spring days that Ohioans live for after a long winter. The sky was painted a turquoise blue. The sun rose like a golden pendant in the sky.

I left my apartment at 11:15 A.M. to give myself plenty of time to get to my 11:55 music appreciation class. To avoid the noon rally, I detoured around campus instead of taking my normal route through the commons. As I walked to the music and speech center, I saw only a handful of students hurrying to classes. Sharp blades of grass broke through the ground that had been covered with snow only a few weeks earlier. Violets and daisies were in bloom, yet an eerie calm hung in the air. An invisible cloud of anxiety and expectation hung over the campus. We all knew something cataclysmic was about to happen, but we had no idea what the magnitude of the event would be.

When I reached the music and speech center, I sank into a seat in the back of the room. Only about a half dozen scared, nervous looking students sat in the classroom. The hands on the wall clock pointed to 11:58. I was only a few minutes late.

I struggled to pay attention to Miss Schubert's lecture on Mozart. A little after noon I heard the clanging of the Victory Bell. Minutes later there was a popping noise outside. Pow! Pow! Pow! It sounded like 4th of July fireworks. We all sat still holding our collective breaths. The noise lasted only for thirteen seconds, but it seemed like a life time.

Miss Schubert paused in mid-sentence and ordered us to stay in our seats. When the noise stopped, she went to the window facing the commons, pulled back the blinds, and peeked out. Turning to the class, she looked like she had seen a ghost. "Class is dismissed," she said.

From the look on her face, I knew something had gone terribly wrong. I grabbed my books and ran to the front exit. Stepping outside, I saw why Miss Schubert's face had turned so pale. All hell had broken loose. A cloud of tear gas choked the air. A crowd of students ran past the building. Fire trucks and ambulances screamed down Main Street.

I stumbled down the stairs. As I stood on the sidewalk feeling disoriented, a white girl ran towards me. "My God, they're killing us," she screamed.

I turned and joined the crowd. It felt as if I was in the middle of a herd of stampeding buffalo. I ran for my life. My leg muscles strained. My heart pounded against my chest like a fist. I ran down Horning Road past apartment buildings, dorms, and houses I passed every day. Only now they seemed surreal.

Finally, I reached my apartment building. Inside, I found Diane sitting cross legged on the living room floor in front of the TV. "Did you hear?" she asked. Her eyes were wide and glassy as marbles. "The guards fired into the crowd. Four students were shot." She burst into tears.

I sat beside her and both of us wept. We wept for our fellow students who had been wounded or killed. We wept for the young soldiers who pulled the triggers. We wept for those who witnessed the tragedy. We wept for ourselves.

On the news we heard that President White had closed the school. The announcer said all students and faculty had to evacuate the university immediately. I didn't know what to do. I tried to call my parents, but the lines were busy. I threw a few things into a suitcase, hugged Diane good-bye, and headed out the door. I was still in shock as I merged with hundreds of students who were heading toward buses, cars, trains, bikes, any mode of transportation they could find leading away from the campus. We were refugees leaving a disaster.

That day I witnessed the second mass exodus from the university. The first one had been a Black student walk out, a troubled sea of dark faces. This one was a student massacre, a river of all colors flooding the campus. Half dazed, I kept moving. About a half dozen school buses waited at the corner. I boarded one heading west.

One Day at the Black and Latino Bookstore

Heading east on Walnut Avenue in Pasadena, California on a sunny winter afternoon, I had one goal in mind, to purchase a box of Christmas cards to send to my family and friends back East. Not just any Christmas cards but cards with pictures of dark angels, Santa Clauses, wise men, and baby Jesuses. Not that there was anything wrong with white Hallmark cards, but I needed positive black images to negate all the negative ones in the media.

Ever since the sixties when I became conscious of black culture, I surrounded myself with black art to strengthen my self esteem and to teach my children that their ancestors weren't just enslaved Africans, but they were healers, artists, engineers, poets, and thinkers. Since then I'd made sending black greeting cards a holiday tradition.

With my four year old son buckled in the passenger's seat of my 1985 Toyota Corolla, I was on a mission. As I neared the corner of Walnut and Mentor, I saw a large crowd blocking the intersection. What on earth was happening? No matter what it was, I wasn't about to let anything deter me. I parked my car in the supermarket lot on Walnut, grabbed my son's hand, and headed back toward Mentor.

The crowd was huge. Two police cars blocked off the entire street all the way south to Colorado Boulevard. With all the holiday events going on, maybe there was a parade or a festival. I headed toward the Black and Latino Bookstore, an independent retailer that catered to readers of black history, economics, religion, science, and sold books and gift items you could never find in a major chain. Owned by an attractive Latino woman named Rita, the establishment had been a fixture in Pasadena for years. Sandwiched between a cluster of small shops and businesses, it was a cozy, inviting place to spend an afternoon.

Holding my son's hand, I elbowed my way through the crowd. When we neared the entrance, a knot of men, women, and children blocked the door. I hoisted my son on my hip and squeezed through a worm hole in the crowd. When I reached the door, it swung open. Looking up, my eyes widened. Hercules towered over me. He stood in the doorway over six feet tall with shoulders so wide he had to turn sideways to exit. I couldn't believe my eyes. It was Muhammad Ali, the boxer I'd had a crush on since I was fifteen!

My mind flashed back to his fights with Sonny Liston, Floyd Patterson, Joe Frazier. I'd seen them all. Loved to see Ali dance across the ring, his feet moving like lightening. I remembered when he threw his Olympic gold medal into the Ohio River because a whites-only restaurant refused to serve him. When he wouldn't fight in Vietnam because, he said, the Vietnamese had never lynched him or call him a nigger. How he stood up, not just for Black Americans, but for all people who had suffered from racial hatred and discrimination.

As he passed by, the crowd parted and started chanting. Ali! Ali! Ali! I chanted with them. His face looked older, more rugged than the Ali of my youth, but he was still strikingly handsome. Watching his powerful physique ascend the stairs to a stage, I hugged my son and shouted, "That's Muhammad Ali. He's the greatest!" My son stared in wonder.

Hwange Sunset

When we headed away from the Hwange Safari Lodge in Zimbabwe at 4 a.m., the sky was pitch black. Slowly, the sun began to rise as we moved away from its well kept lodgings, gardens, and pools. Bumping down a narrow dirt road in the back seat of a Land Cruiser, I wondered why the locals called the national reserve the bush. It was absolutely breathtaking, stretching brown and gold for miles surrounding the lodge where my friend and publisher Leon Knight, had booked his editor, George, and me a two night stay. The weather was perfect, seventy degrees and sunny. Beyond tall scrubby bushes and acacia trees we could see the savanna. In some spots thick foliage blocked our view but in others it was like looking through a panoramic window.

This was my first safari and it was more spectacular than I ever imagined. As I gazed at a giraffe ambling on long twiggy legs across the savanna, the hair stood on the back of my neck. Our driver, Tunde, kept us entertained with amusing stories about the wildlife. We rode all day staring through binoculars at black rhinos, lions, leopards, and buffalo; all of the big five except one, the African elephant.

"I can't believe we didn't see one elephant," Leon, a large, bearded white man, grumbled as we headed back to the lodge in the evening. I was a little disappointed too, but how could I complain after seeing so many regal creatures in their own habitat?

We were about a mile away from the lodge when Tunde pressed his foot on the brake. "Look behind you, slowly," he said.

I turned and stared. Towering about ten yards behind us in the middle of the road was the largest creature I had ever seen. Standing at least ten feet tall with great ivory tusks, a long trunk, and banana leaf like ears, it was prehistoric! My heart beat like a drum. Time stood still. The enormous pachyderm lifted its right foot, raised its trunk, and fanned its ears. *Oh, my*

God, it's going to charge, I thought. I wanted to yell at Tunde to go, but my lips wouldn't move. Seconds later, the mammoth lowered its trunk, turned, and disappeared in the bush with the setting sun.

References

Titles listed below have previously appeared in the following publications:

"Lessons from an Evergreen" and "A Cartoon Matinee" first appeared in the *Altadena Poetry Review Anthology* 2019 (Shabda Press).

"Sand Drawing" and "Meditation on a Supermoon" first appeared in the *Altadena Poetry Review Anthology* 2018 (Golden Foothills Press).

"Your Words and Actions Do Matter" first appeared in the *Journal of Modern Poetry 21* (2018, Chicago Poetry Press).

"The Drinking Gourd" and "Meditation on a Supermoon" first appeared in the *Journal of Modern Poetry 20* (2017, Chicago Poetry Press).

"Sonny" first appeared in *Coiled Serpent: Poets Arising from the Cultural Quakes & Shifts of Los Angeles* (2016, Tia Chucha Press).

"Happy Hour" and "A Little Watering" first appeared in the *Altadena Poetry Review Anthology 2015* (2015, Golden Foothills Press).

"Blood on the Commons: Kent State Massacre" first appeared in *Crossing the River Ohio* (2014, JAH Light Communications).

"I am Woman" first appeared in *Deep River Rhythms* (2002, Sunji Ali, Publisher).

"Love Letter to Grandpa" first appeared in *Grand Fathers* (1999, Henry, Holt & Company, Inc.).

"Love Equation" first appeared in *A Rock Against the Wind* (1996, The Berkeley Publishing Group).

"Uncle Cal" first appeared in *River Crossings Voices of the Diaspora* (1994, International Black Writers & Artists, Los Angeles).

"Red Moon" first appeared in *High Performance* magazine, (Summer, 1992 18th Street Arts Complex, Santa Monica, CA).

"The Blues" and "Mystery Lover" first appeared in *In the Company of Poets* (December, 1991 in the Company of Poets, Oakland, CA.)

www.ingramcontent.com/pod-product-compliance
Lightning Source LLC
Chambersburg PA
CBHW032132090426
42743CB00007B/573